# For My Daughter

If it is true that we are judged
By the deeds of the child we bear,
Then I shall truly be a king
When judgement day is here.

George E. Young

*Presented to:*

Elizabeth Marsh Newcomb

My darling daughter

*By:*

Whom is so warm

careing and Appreciative

*Date:* May 1, 1989

*Special Message:*

_____

_____

_____

_____

_____

_____

_____

_____

_____

THIS BOOK IS DEDICATED with love to my wonderful wife, Marcie, and her lovely daughter, Cherie Banks Hirsch.

# ACKNOWLEDGMENTS

To Carl E. and Margaret Anne (Johnny) Alleman, who have been in many ways the best father and mother this author could ever have. The direct and indirect influence they both have had on the life of the author and on the text of this book is substantial.

To my wife, Marcie Young, and to Samuel L. Hornbeak for providing this author with a constant living example of the love, ethics and values that bring true meaning to life.

To the many friends and parents who willingly presented their views, feelings and memories to the author and provided the insight and inspiration for the text of this book.

# TABLE OF CONTENTS

# PREFACE

The author of this book does not claim to be an accomplished writer, scholar, philosopher or poet. He is simply a father.

It is the author's hope that through this book other parents will find it possible to communicate thoughts and feelings to their daughters for which words were not before available.

The special messages expressed herein are applicable to daughters of all ages. Whether read by a young girl or a mature woman, these messages should be easily understood and remembered. Since the verses make no reference to dates, terminologies or events pertinent to any specific era, the credence of this book's contents should be preserved for generations to come.

This book is divided into three sections, each dealing with a special and important relationship. The first section deals with the parent/daughter relationship in an effort to communicate and clarify the feelings and emotions involved in that relationship. The second section deals with perspective ... the relationship that events of today have with the whole of one's life. The third section addresses the relationship that our personal values and priorities have to our lasting happiness.

Though references to theology have been purposely omitted in recognition and respect for varying religious beliefs, the values and principles expressed herein should parallel and compliment the teachings of most organized religions.

Those who receive this book are fortunate, for someone cared enough to give it. Whether actually from a parent, or from another who truly cares, the gift of this book says that the one receiving it is very special.

Section One

# THE PARENT/DAUGHTER RELATIONSHIP

*The relationship that exists between a parent and his or her daughter is a powerful and unique bond. The effect this relationship has on both the parent and the daughter is deep and lasting, yet the very essence of the relationship is often misunderstood.*

*Being a good parent is a rewarding, yet very difficult task, as is being a good daughter. There are no schools that can adequately prepare either for the wonderful roles they have. They must learn as they go. They each will make mistakes.*

*Unlike most relationships, the one between a parent and child begins with deep mutual love and admiration; a love and admiration that is difficult to destroy and can evolve into a lasting and wonderful friendship. As each begins to grow in their role, they begin to realize that the other has faults and weaknesses. There are periods where the goals, desires and attitudes of one may seem foreign to the other. An understanding of these differences is essential.*

*It is the degree of understanding that determines the effectiveness of our relationships . . . understanding each other . . . understanding understanding . . . understanding misunderstanding. The only way to truly understand is to communicate; to address differences, to tell and show our feelings, to explore misunderstandings together.*

*The verses that follow communicate feelings that most parents have . . . feelings that promote understanding . . . feelings that are rarely, if ever, expressed.*

1

# YOUR FRIEND

Sometimes it's hard to write the words
That you, my dear, should see.
Or say the things you need to hear,
Or be as I should be.

You grow so fast and learn so much
It's hard for me each day,
To say or do just what is best
To help along the way.

Should I be silent or give advice?
Should I answer yes or no?
Should I have control — set many rules,
Or simply let you go?

One thing is certain . . . I'll make mistakes,
And some'll seem hard to mend.
*But if nothing else seems clear right now,*
*Please know that I'm your friend.*

# THINGS THAT MATTER

It's often hard to understand
 From where the other comes.
It may seem as if we're marching
 To the beat of different drums.

The songs I like, some things I do,
 The way I cut my hair,
Must seem to you as very dull
 Just as the clothes I wear.

Your youth is now . . . a different day
 Than days when I was young.
Some things I never dreamed would be
 Are things you live among.

*But all the things that matter, dear,*
 *Are still the same today.*
*If only those we understand,*
 *The rest shall fade away.*

# UNSURPASSED PLEASURE

It's rainy and cold. It's been a long day.
   You're as tired as you've ever been.
Your feet are wet and you're chilled to the bone,
   But you're finally at home again.

The evening is yours . . . whatever you wish;
   A warm, bubbly bath's your desire.
Then in your robe — hot chocolate in hand —
   You cuddle-up by a roaring fire.

That kind of pleasure may seem unsurpassed,
   But it doesn't compare with this . . .
*Just think of the pleasure parents must feel*
   *When their daughter gives 'em a kiss.*

# BRIDGING THE GAP

You were a wee little girl upon my lap
When I first feared the generation gap.
I swore it would never exist with us.
"Not between me and this cute little cuss".

I tried to stay young and to know your ways;
To learn to appreciate whatever's the craze,
But soon I found that I appear a sap
When I'm on your side of the generation gap.

By the same token, you just wouldn't be you
If you did things the same as I used to do.
So let's face one thing, there's certainly a gap.
It was planned to be so. It's not a mishap.

It wouldn't be good to look the other way
And pretend that gap doesn't exist today.
Let's explore that gap and try to find out
Just what the other side is all about.

If I can understand from where you come
And let you know where I'm coming from,
*Then though time put us on a different ridge,*
*Mutual understanding will be our bridge.*

# A BIT MORE CREDIT

"If only parents could understand!"
  You must think that quite a lot.
And sometimes, dear, we wish we could,
  Cause perfect we are not.

But perhaps a bit more credit is due
  Once all the data's compiled,
*For you've not been a parent as yet,*
  *But we were once a child.*

# FOR YOU I WISH

I wish for you a contented life
Filled with love and grace.
For there is no greater joy for me
Than a smile upon your face.
But when times get hard and you feel pain,
I hope that all your pride
Won't keep me from where I'd want to be,
And that is by your side.

I wish for you a life of great wealth
If that's for what you yearn.
But if it's not, I'll be just as proud
No matter what you earn.
For you see, my dear, it's not those things
That set some folks apart.
It's not what's in your bank account,
But what's truly in your heart.

I wish for you a life of your own . . .
The way you want it to be.
The path you choose and where it may lead
Will not be up to me.
*Wherever you go, whatever you become,*
*No matter what you do.*
*You'll always have my love and support.*
*I wish the best for you.*

# UNCONDITIONAL LOVE

Remember, dear, when you're a success,
  I'll be happy as can be.
But remember, too, that when you fail,
  You can always come to me.

There's little in life we cannot share.
  We'll share the bad times, too.
*For my love has no conditions, dear,*
  *That's what I give to you.*

# SHARING

When I remember my younger days,
My heart goes out to you.
Cause I remember problems I had
That all young folks go through.

I'd do things wrong, or get in trouble,
Or make a bad grade in school.
Friends would do things that hurt my feelings.
I'd be embarrassed, be a fool.

My heart was broken over loves I lost.
At times I felt lonely and sad.
So you see, my dear, most problems you have
Were at one time those that I had.

Being a parent means helping your child,
Cause growing up is hard to do.
Sharing successes is part of the joy.
So is sharing the problems, too.

I want you to do the things that are right,
Like I try to teach you to do.
But it won't always happen and I know that.
I once was a young person, too.

*If you make a mistake or simply feel sad,*
*Nothing could make my day as bright,*
*As your saying to me; "I have a problem.*
*Can you help me make it alright?".*

# BEWARE THE SHADOW

My shadow, daughter, of it beware.
Don't linger where it's laid.
The woman you can be, like a lovely flower,
Won't grow well in the shade.

## YOU ARE YOU & I AM ME

I hope you know I'm not the person
   That I want you to be.
It's important for you to realize
   You are you and I am me.

There are faults I have and deeds I've done
   I'd never wish for you.
But those can be your greatest lessons
   Of what to or not to do.

# REGRETTABLE TIMES

You're home from school, you have things to say,
  And you find that I'm not there.
You have some problem and need to talk,
  But I'm still at work somewhere.

Oh, how I'd love to have shared those times.
  Somehow it doesn't seem fair . . .
*That the only times I now regret*
  *Are the times I wasn't there.*

## IF IT WEREN'T FOR YOU

It's often so rough, this being a parent,
   That if it weren't for you,
I just don't think that I would be able
   To ever make it through.

SECTION TWO

# PERSPECTIVE

*One essential key to a truly happy life is the acquired ability to put one's life in proper perspective . . . to measure the importance of today's events in relation to the whole of our lives. It is this ability that can help us to establish our priorities and keep them in order . . . to keep our values intact, our attitude positive and our sense of humor about us.*

*Whether it's a pimple on your cheek the night of the prom or the death of a loved one; whether a serious illness, a fallen career, a divorce or a failing grade in school; troubles, disappointments and hardships are a major part of every life. How we accept and react to such events can well determine our overall happiness, as well as what kind of person we eventually become.*

*The happiest women learn to look past the moment, to appreciate and make the most of what they have and to always see the brightest side. They are strong enough to begin again and wise enough to learn much from what has happened. . . .*

# FINDING THE BEST

Life is fun, but it's sometimes hard.
  It's difficult to comprehend
Why some things happen and some things don't,
  Why some things have to end.

Don't try too hard to understand.
  Don't confuse yourself with why.
*Just find the best in every minute.*
  *It's there if you'll just try.*

# BAD DAYS?

It's easy to think some days are bad
While others are lots of fun.
Some never appreciate every day
Till they almost miss just one.

# TROUBLES

"Nobody knows the troubles I know."
  That's a lot of bull!
Compared to the problems many folks have
  Ours are rather dull.

# BEYOND WHAT'S SEEN

Does the sun come up in the early morn
   And fall in the west at night?
Are things always as they appear to be?
   Is our perspective right?

A revolving earth brings the sun in view.
   The sun doesn't fall or rise.
What first we see's not always what's there.
   There's more than meets the eyes.

In every misfortune that comes our way
   A blessing can be found.
There is good no matter where we are
   If we'll just look around.

The happiest people look beyond what's seen
   Till the bright side is in view.
*Is your glass half empty or is it half full?*
   *That is totally up to you.*

# COUNTING YOUR SHEEP

Problems, as my companions, may . . .
Be with me through most of the day,
But blessings are the little sheep
I count at night to go to sleep.

# THE EXCEPTIONAL GAL

When a joke is told or a prank is pulled
Even lowly women can grin.
For humor, then, is so easy to find.
It's not hidden somewhere within.

The common woman can look to the past
And laugh about things she sees.
Cause the hurt is gone and who cares now?
Those are only old memories.

The exceptional gal can laugh at a mirror
And take life's worst with a smile.
*She's the one who finds humor in everyday life.*
*It's that kind of gal who has style.*

*. . . The relationship that today has with the rest of our lives is a complex and often misunderstood relationship, for none of us know what tomorrow will bring. Some understanding can be gained, however, by reviewing a portion of life's normal cycle and some of the stages through which we each must pass.*

*An infant is brought into life totally dependent on others for survival and happiness. With no thought of tomorrow, her physical comfort, food and love seem her only concern.*

*Every passing day brings the infant new abilities, new challenges and a little less dependency. Soon, as a pre-schooler, the average child in our country now assumes that a degree of physical comfort and nourishment will be provided. She discovers new joys and develops new desires. The new toy, the upcoming Christmas, the hug of approval from mom and dad; these make up her dreams.*

*The preschooler has a seemingly simple life. Her basic needs are provided by others, yet natural disappointments, frustrations and hurts loom as major catastrophes, bringing grief to her life. How is the pre-school child to know that the hurt of a skinned knee will soon heal, that the scolding was given only out of love or that the broken toy will not affect the whole of her life?*

*Soon reaching adolescence, the growing child begins to feel independence, yet still must be dependent. Since more and more time is spent away from home, mom's or dad's approval is no longer enough. The desire to fit in with her peers becomes a primary motivation.*

*Now at an awkward stage between childhood and womanhood, the adolescent has sexual urges and feels her body changing. Some bodies mature earlier than others, causing some adolescents embarrassment over a girlish appearance while others appear more "womanly." The pressures to be a "woman" or to be grown-up are felt for the first time during adolescence.*

22

*Her thoughts are preoccupied with the boy in class, getting a driver's license, the prom, school grades, summer vacation, the party next week, maturing physically, the big game, what mom and dad will think or do, the school tryouts, but most of all, with fitting in and being accepted. Everything that happens seems all-important. Small events take on giant proportions. It is at this stage that young people begin to deal more independently with loneliness, rejection, male and female relationships, leadership, success, embarrassment, shame and a host of other emotions.*

*Like the pre-schooler whose broken toy seems a catastrophic event, how is the adolescent to know that her hurts will soon fade? How is she to know that soon nobody will care if the big game was won or if she fit in? How is she to know that those problems she hides inside are the same ones that mom and dad had? How does she know that those things she does to "fit in" or gain acceptance may well cost her dearly for the rest of her life? How does she know how to put life in perspective? . . .*

# THAT MYTHICAL CRYSTAL BALL

I wish you had a crystal ball,
But not to see tomorrow...
To go there and look back at now
To better gauge your sorrow.

The weight of grief can crush a girl
If she can't look past today,
But grief's like ice and time's the heat
That melts such weight away.

*That sadness, dear, that breaks your heart*
*Might'nt seem so big at all,*
*If you could see it in perspective*
*Through that mythical crystal ball.*

# BEYOND

The football game is very close.
The score is tied at three.
The final pass is in the air.
What will the outcome be?

Whether leading cheers from the field
Or sitting in the stands.
Whether cheering as a pom-pon girl
Or marching with the bands.

*It is you, my dear, and only you*
*Who determines what shall be.*
*For this game is but one score in life.*
*It's beyond that you must see.*

# DAYS AT MUFORD HIGH

On a day much like today, at a high school very near,
There were four boys and a girl attending school.
The first, we'll call him Jim, was the hero every year.
He was the star of every sport . . . a mister cool.

Another we'll call Bob was most likely for success.
Every year he was a leader in his class.
The third guy was a party boy, the one they all called Jess.
He was a laugh-a-minute guy, but kinda crass.

It was Ernie who was odd and always seemed alone.
He wore funny clothes and never quite fit in.
The girl nobody knew, but we know her name was Joan.
Now, the story 'bout these folks we can begin.

Graduation came and passed, and as the years went by
The differences between them weren't so great.
Nobody seemed to care about their days at Muford High.
How they were back then was now quite out-of-date.

Jim learned that when he bragged of scores he then had made,
People yawned and most considered him a bore.
And even good ole' Jess had to learn himself a trade,
Cause the world was not just parties anymore.

Nobody cares today if Ernie couldn't get a date,
Or if Bob got all the votes at Muford High.
*It's what they are and what they learned that'll make 'em great,*
*Not what they were in childhood days gone by.*

To rest upon their laurels or to dwell on weaker traits
Will stop anyone from being fully grown.
The point this story makes is that all them can be great.
In fact, the ending has them working all for Joan.

# FITTING IN

It's human nature to want to fit in,
But how low will you have to stoop?
What is the price of fitting in?
How important is the group?

These questions are very important to you,
So answer 'em before you say yes
To something a group expects you to do,
Or to someone you want to impress.

Tis the last of these questions that seems most hard,
Cause importance relates to time.
What now seems important to you or the group
Might later be worth not a dime.

Besides, my darling, that group's gonna fade.
They'll grow and go their own way.
*The woman you become by saying no*
*Is the woman with whom you will stay.*

# THE IMPRESSEE

If you must do or say something that's wrong
    To impress someone you see,
Then to be an impressor is not for you
    And neither's the impressee.

# JUST LISTEN

If you want someone's friendship
Then while you both walk,
Just keep your mouth closed
And try not to talk.
  Just listen.

It is strange how people
Will think you so wise
When you don't say a thing,
But speak with your eyes
  And just listen.

*Two ears and one mouth*
*Was for us a good start.*
*When used in proportion*
*We become twice as smart,*
  So just listen.

# AN EXPENSIVE SPORT

It's great to see you laugh and play,
    To know you're having fun.
But fun can be an expensive sport
    If it isn't wisely done.

Ask yourself some questions first,
    And use your common sense.
Is the fun you plan gonna be done
    At another person's expense?

Or maybe if you think a while,
    And the consequence you weigh,
You may learn it could be you
    That just might have to pay.

In any prison or graveyard
    I'll show you more than one
Who's there because she didn't weigh
    The cost of unwise fun.

Don't get me wrong, there is lots of fun
    A girl can have today,
But the only fun that's really fun's
    When no one has to pay.

So think before you do that thing
    That might best be left undone.
*Cause fun does not make happiness,*
    *But happiness is lots of fun.*

# PLAYING WITH OUR FUTURE

Our greatest resource lies in our youth.
   That resource we must protect.
It isn't just up to us older folks
   To show our children respect.

When once on a date or with some friends,
   It could be something you did
That had an effect on some young person
   And changed the life of a kid.

How the world will be depends on its youth.
   That's a truth and not a myth.
*When a young girl plays with other children,*
   *It's our future she's playing with.*

# TOMORROW'S LEADER

Any girl can say yes to everything
  And simply drift along with the flow,
*But the woman who will lead in years ahead*
  *Is woman enough now to say no.*

# GROWING

A growing girl may see another
Who's exactly her own age
Who seems to be a whole lot older;
To have reached another stage.

It is true that some girls develop fast
And others develop slow.
*But when you're a woman isn't determined*
*By how fast a body will grow.*

33

*. . . Having passed through adolescence, the young adult carries both pride in her successes and scars from many hurts. Some have become mature women at this stage while others are still girls in a mature body. None are yet the women they will someday be.*

*The young adult now has different pressures and concerns. Choosing a career, becoming "successful", buying a car, getting married, starting a family, paying bills, learning a trade and other such things now occupy her thoughts. Very often the young adult is still preoccupied with trying to "fit in" and prove herself to others. She often feels that lots of money or position will prove her "success" and that marrying an attractive man will somehow prove her "womanhood."*

*How is this young adult to know what will bring her true happiness? What is "success" and how is it achieved? What qualities are really important in a husband? What should her priorities be? How does she put life in perspective? . . .*

# WHAT'S THE SENSE?

No matter what kind of sense you have:
Sense or scents or cents.
The kind of sense to cherish most
Is good ole' common sense.

## DOING

An education will make you smart.
It's something a woman should prize.
But schooling, dear, is just a start.
It's experience that makes one wise.

You can spend years with theories galore,
Looking through rose colored glasses.
*But one year of doing will teach you more*
*Than a decade spent in classes.*

# A TIME TO WAIT

What a wonderful thing, to be in love;
   To "know" that guy's for you.
But what a shame that so many young girls
   Hurry so to say "I do".

It is true, my dear, that charm can deceive.
   Good looks will soon fade away.
It's the love for things that will always be
   That wise young women will weigh.

Does he have love and peace and self-control?
   Is he kind and patient, too?
Is he faithful and good and full of joy?
   Is he truly in love with you?

If your answers are yes and you love him,
   Then once you decide to wed,
*Why not wait one more year, just to make sure,*
   *Before those vows are said?*

For better, for worse — In sickness or health.
   Your commitment is for life.
It's an awesome decision that a woman makes
   The day she becomes a wife.

# TRUST

It is much better to live
In a tent if you must
Than to live in a mansion
With a man you can't trust.

# THE TURTLE AND US

There are many things that limit folks
  And make an old woman cry,
But none as sure as when she knows
  That she didn't even try.

No-one who tries can a failure be,
  At least not in my eyes.
The only one I'd call a failure
  Is the one who never tries.

*Our life's much like the turtle's life,*
  *For if its moves you'll check,*
*It never takes one step ahead*
  *Till it first sticks out its neck.*

# IT MUST BE WHAT THEY "ATE"

**Successful women** will innovate,
Originate and initiate.

They conjugate, congregate,
cogitate and meditate.

They incorporate, speculate,
consolidate and syndicate.

They coronate, inaugurate,
abdicate and dedicate.

They emancipate, liberate,
integrate and emigrate.

They legislate, adjudicate,
litigate and vindicate.

They investigate, estimate,
calculate and tabulate.

They medicate, inoculate,
sanitate and operate.

They titillate, infatuate,
stimulate and propagate.

They aviate, navigate,
fabricate and duplicate.

They cooperate, participate,
coordinate and tolerate.

They communicate, negotiate,
mediate and arbitrate.

They cultivate, excavate,
irrigate and compensate.

They appreciate, congratulate,
celebrate and elaborate.

They perforate, penetrate,
appropriate and captivate.

They educate, graduate,
concentrate and hesitate.

They regulate, delegate,
generate and terminate.

They reiterate, anticipate,
mitigate and simulate.

**Others** simply procrastinate.

# PROCRASTINATION

The only thing between here
And your destination
Is that time-eating monster
called procrastination.

# THE CREATURE IN DISGUISE

There are conflicting rumors that are spreading around
About some kind of creatures that are roaming this ground.
There are big ones and small ones, they say, everywhere.
But just what they look like, no one is aware.

Some think they are mean, cause I've heard many cases
Where they jump up and slap folks right in their faces.
Yet victims never see 'em cause to this day they swear
That the illusive creatures just never were there.

If you don't grab 'em quick when they first come near
They will go like a flash and never reappear.
There are thousands of schools that train us to find 'em
And wonderful bounties for those who can bind 'em.

Rumors say they look small when coming your way,
But they look a lot bigger when going away.
They often wear disguises and hide in the dark.
To find them takes working, one man did remark.

I've heard of some hunting them all of their days.
Others just wait for them as if in a daze.
Some lucky folks do have them knock at their door,
But most the shy creatures knock once and no more.

Rumors conflict, but in one thing there's unity.
When the creatures were named, they were named opportunity.
So if you never see one, don't sit there and moan.
*You can get off your backside and create your own.*

43

# CONTROL

Your future, your career,
Your happiness, too,
Cannot be controlled
Till you first control you.

*. . . Like adolescence, the period of middleage is often one of crises. Some women are well on their way to fulfilling the dreams they had as a young woman. Others are not. It is at this stage that some women begin looking back as much as ahead. Perhaps they're not where they wanted to be. Perhaps they have the career success they thought was so important, but family or health problems minimize the importance of that success.*

*Did they give up too much for the things they have? How do they find happiness now? What is really important? Have their values and/or priorities been wrong? How should they change their lives? How can they change?*

*Sadly, it is at this stage that many women first turn to the true values in life and begin to discover what is really important. Some reset their goals and become contented with less . . . only to find that they really have much more.*

*How were they to have known?*

# A PAIN IN THE NECK

Looking back causes a pain in the neck
For those who do it a lot.
"If I'da done this." or "If I'da done that."
Won't getcha anymore than you got.

# TAKING YOUR MEDICINE

There are many things we all must accept . . .
  Things in life that'll always exist.
There's weather and taxes and physical things,
  But blame's at the top of the list.

Most will accept anyone's thanks,
  And credit we're happy to claim.
But when things go wrong, how many folks
  Are willing to accept the blame?

"It was Janet's fault." or "I couldn't help it."
  Or "Look what you made me do!"
Those are common phrases we hear every day.
  Accepting the blame is taboo.

What about that mistake you recently made
  For which you now feel shame?
Will you let it just fester and grow inside,
  Or stand up and take the blame?

Keeping shame inside is like a bad disease.
  It can make anyone feel sick.
*Like a dose of medicine is blame, my dear,*
  *It's better if you take it quick.*

It's easy to blame others for what goes wrong,
  Or face the blame some later day.
But to stand up now and admit it's your fault
  Is by far the wiser way.

# VALUES & PRIORITIES

*Everyone has goals, dreams and aspirations. What seems to separate the happy people from the unhappy ones is not so much whether dreams are fulfilled; nor does it seem to be material possessions, physical traits or intelligence level. Have you ever wondered how some can be so happy with what seems to be so little, or how some who appear to have so much manage to be so unhappy?*

*To better understand how true happiness can be achieved, perhaps one should explore what it is that can make us unhappy. Unhappiness always stems from a loss of some kind . . . a loss of something deemed important.*

*The most obvious type of loss is the more outward kind . . . the loss of a dream or desire that never materialized, the loss of affection or love from a friend or spouse, the loss of possessions, the loss of youth for an athlete, the loss of a loved one. Such losses, often unpreventable, will happen in every life. How we react is largely dependent on our perspective of life. That perspective is often determined by the priorities we establish for ourselves. If that thing that is lost is a high priority in our life, such a loss can be devastating.*

*What of the businesswoman who loses her fortune in a business transaction? What of the woman who reaches middle-age only to realize that the life about which she always dreamed will simply never be? What of the young lover who loses her guy to another? What do they now have left? What were their priorities?*

*What are the material or external things you want in life? Will they bring you lasting happiness? Perhaps it is more pertinent to ask if you can have that happiness without those things. Do you own your dreams or do they own you? Where are these things in your priorities?*

*There are many things in life that cannot be taken away. The happiest of women keep these as their priorities. Others often give them away in pursuit of dreams they feel are more important. It is the loss of these things that will surely bring unhappiness.*

*One such loss is that of your pride, self-worth and self-esteem. The young woman who turns to drugs, for instance, because "fitting-in" with some group is one of her top priorities will eventually think less of herself. Some of her self-esteem will vanish. When that group is gone, what is left? Should "fitting-in" have been a top priority? Her convictions, her values and her self-esteem will someday be far more important, but how was she to have known?*

*Another such internal and preventable loss is, perhaps, the number-one cause of unhappiness in our country . . . the loss of our inner peace. Hatred, jealousy, bitterness, envy, intolerance, spite and other such emotions can rob us of our inner peace and hence of our happiness.*

*Perhaps that happy woman who appears to have so very little has more than meets the eye. Perhaps she kept those things that others gave away. Perhaps she kept her convictions and her values intact, thus keeping her self-esteem. Perhaps she kept her sense of humor and developed love for the people and beautiful things that surround her, thus keeping her inner peace. Perhaps these were her priorities.*

*A woman with those priorities is free. She is free to seek all the dreams, material items and worldly pleasures she wishes without risk of them possessing her. She can care about all people, but no care will own her. She will suffer loss, sorrow, disappointment and sadness like other people, but she will emerge with her happiness and her sense of humor intact. Such a woman is a blessed woman.*

# DREAMS

People's dreams have made this land
  A special place to live.
Hope and joy and goals for life
  Are things a dream can give.

*So dream, my dear, but heed these words:*
  *Dreams can spell disaster*
*When you stop smelling that tiny rose,*
  *And dreams become your master.*

# THINGS

To seek your pleasure from things you own
Whether many things or few,
Can add spice to life and bring some joy
Until those things own you.

# OVERLOOKED PLEASURES

The greatest of pleasures
For you and for me
Are often overlooked
Because they are free.

# THE ROAD TO HAPPINESS

That illusive place called happiness
    Is sought by many women.
Let's review the journey they make
    And where those women have been.

Many started on their journey
    Quite early in their years.
Some tell gruesome stories about
    A road that's filled with tears.

They speak of fog that settled in
    So they couldn't see ahead;
How some roads seemed completely blocked
    By the waters storms had shed.

They talk of signs along the road
    That led some folks astray;
Of laughing fools at every turn
    Who promise a better way.

Some took wrong turns, were lost for years.
    Some never made it back.
It seemed the roads that looked most smooth
    Were ones that went off-track.

I heard of times they had to tread
    Where no road had been cut.
Of lonely, boring years they spent
    Just plodding in a rut.

Some saw mirages just ahead . . .
    Thought happiness was there.
But when they reached the spot they saw,
    They found that spot was bare.

They told of bandits they couldn't see
  Who would rob them of their souls;
Of people disguised as kindly friends
  Offering fruit in poison bowls.

No matter how tough the journey was
  Those arriving always said,
They learned to see in darkest of times
  And to find the light ahead.

When describing the road they all agreed
  That it went clear around.
It was the very same place they started
  That happiness was found.

Many years were wasted by some of them.
  They suffered needless strife,
*Cause happiness is no destination, dear,*
  *It's a daily way of life.*

# THE THIEF OF HAPPINESS

Think of cold and what it really is.
    Tis only the absence of heat.
It grows much easier for us to feel
    The more warmth does retreat.
Hate is like cold; It cannot be felt
    Till something is taken away.
It's absence of love that brings on hate.
    That is a heavy price to pay.

For instance, if one has genuine love
    For the things she does each day,
And also has love for every person
    Whom she meets along the way.
If she finds the good in everything
    And in every person, too,
Her love will bring her much happiness
    And her sorrows will be few.

Now, take that woman — remove some love —
    Make her thoughts less kind.
Do you think that she's as happy now
    With her new frame of mind?
*You see, my dear, hate is like cold.*
    *A bitter feeling it makes.*
*Some love must go before hate moves in,*
    *And that your happiness takes.*

# A WEALTHY WOMAN

The woman who has pride and peace of mind
  And the respect of many men . . .

The woman who says in her twilight years
  That she'd do it all again . . .

The woman who loves the flowers and trees
  And watching the animals play . . .

She's a wealthy woman, for what she has
  Can never be taken away.

# ABILITIES

If I could list for you, dear, what skills to acquire . . .
  The abilities I think are key.
The list I'd make would look something like this.
  It's these that can make a girl free.

The ability to:

  Face disagreement without feeling disagreeable.
  Be alone without feeling lonely.
  Be doubted without having doubts.
  Lose without suffering loss.
  Try without feeling foolish.
  Be judged without judging.
  Own without being owned.
  Care without caring too much.
  Fail without being a failure.
  Be lied about without dealing in lies.
  Succeed without feeling superior.
  Say no without fear of rejection.
  Think well of yourself and not be bound
    by other's thoughts.
  Wait and not be tired by waiting.
  Pursue dreams without them pursuing you.
  Love, yet not let love destroy you.
  Choose friends without fear of not being chosen.
  Help others without known reward.
  Witness dishonesty, yet not be dishonest.
  Be yourself and then be proud you were.

# IN COMPARISON

When I graded myself from one to ten
Compared to others I know,
In every category someone was better.
My grades were always too low.

So I quit doing that and changed my ways.
I am happier now than then.
*If I'm better today than I was before*
*I simply give myself a ten.*

# THE GIFT OF TIME

If everyone received their pay
The day they were given birth,
The wise ones would invest it well
And build upon their worth.

The foolish ones would waste their wealth
And squander their every cent,
Then someday beg for one more dime
Cause their fortune they have spent.

We did receive that gift at birth.
Our pay was precious time.
Since we never know how much we have,
Every minute should be prime.

Each day is like a dollar, dear,
When you spend it, it is gone.
But when that day's invested wise,
Many great things it can spawn.

*The rest of your life begins right now.*
*What a very special day!*
*Twenty-four hours for you to invest*
*So that every hour will pay.*

# THE TIME TILL THEN

If a year from now seems a long, long time,
   And next month seems far away,
Then tell me, dear, where last month has gone,
   Why last year's like yesterday.

Patience is taught by the history of time;
   By taking a look at its past.
Like the days before that went fleeting by,
   The days ahead will go fast.

People think they can't wait till a week from now
   When a wonderful thing is foreseen,
*But the very best part of a week from now's*
   *Seven days to enjoy in between.*

# YOUR LONG-TERM ADDRESS

It's strange how some will give such great care
To the house their body lives in,
Yet mistreat and abuse that marvelous place:
The body their soul is in.

Some spend their fortunes to buy a house.
It's a symbol of their wealth.
Such comforts mean little to any of them
If they've also spent their health.

So ponder this question: Where do you live?
But think before venturing a guess.
*That number and street belong to a house.*
*Your body's your long-term address.*

# A SELF-ASSURING THOUGHT

If your luck is good, the day will come
  When you'll be old and grey.
Perhaps it's time you looked ahead
  To the thoughts you'll have that day.

You'll think of times you laughed so hard
  Your side began to ache,
And times you cried yourself to sleep,
  Your heart about to break.

The fun you had, mistakes you made,
  And dreams you had to chase.
The loves you lost, those childhood friends,
  That special little place.

*All those thoughts you will have, my dear,*
  *But none will be so blest*
*As that downright self-assuring thought*
  *That you did your very best.*

# A FRIEND'S FRIENDS

There's very little that'll stop your growth
 Or restrict your thinking more,
Than to limit your circle to those of one kind
 And to others shut the door.

Some very fine people whose paths you'll cross
 Won't be a bit like you.
They'll dress and act and look much different
 And not do the things you do.

Being their friend isn't always so easy.
 Others you know may object.
But in the end you'll broaden your circle
 And gain everybody's respect.

Even one who's a friend to everyone
 Won't have everyone as a friend,
*But the one who's a friend to everyone*
 *Has many more friends in the end.*

# THE PROPER VIEW

We all can love the good times
  Or beauty in the sky above,
Or embrace a friend who helped us.
  That's the easy kind of love.

But what of the ones who bring us harm?
  Is there beauty in them too?
Finding love for the ones who hurt us
  Is a difficult thing to do.

There are many things to understand.
  Many which we never will.
But always try hard to understand
  That ones who mean us ill.

Tis easy to hate or to judge those folks,
  To seek revenge or fight.
But conflict brings us certain grief,
  So why not set things right?

To understand such people as these
  Our eyes and ears won't do.
*It's through a loving heart we must see*
  *To gain the proper view.*

# GREATEST OF WOMEN

The greatest of women
Are common women,
Born of kings or no.

They can dine with the rich,
Mingle with the poor,
And those in between they know.

# THE OTHER VIEW

Even small people have opinions.
  To them each issue's clear.
When another view is stated,
  Small folks never hear.

Common people have opinions.
  They know that theirs is right.
When opposing views are spoken,
  They'll argue, even fight.

Great people also have opinions,
  But are not afraid to grow.
They listen with an open mind
  And learn what others know.

If you have respect for others' views
  And never shut them out,
You'll learn far more than issues, dear,
  You'll learn what folks are about.

You needn't agree with everything said,
  But listen whenever you can.
*For nothing will ever serve you more*
  *Than understanding fellow man.*

# THE SMALLEST MIND

The smallest of minds is the narrow mind,
    And notice what it abuts.
It is usually located just above
    A mouth that seldom shuts.

# YOUR DAILY PORTRAIT

Great people speak of ideals and truths.
Principles are their thrust.
They see the good in everybody.
Such people we can trust.

Common folks speak of things and events,
Happenings, and not much more.
They pick their friends from one select group.
They're the ones we all know next door.

Lowly people speak of other people,
Finding fault whenever they can.
They play people against one another,
And have since time began.

*One can tell more by what you speak*
*Than the words that you utter may say.*
*Your tongue is your brush, your words your palette,*
*And your portrait you paint every day.*

# CURSE OR GIFT

We split tiny atoms and land on the moon.
  We get energy out of a hole.
Yet the most powerful thing that we ever had
  Runs rampant and out of control.

  It's the most awesome weapon known to man.
  It's begun every war that time has span.
  It's injured more people and caused more pain
  Than the atomic bomb or the fighter plane.
  It causes despair. It causes deceit.
  It leads us astray and shows our conceit.
  It makes enemies and fabricates lies.
  It's often quite filthy and it terrifies.

If we could only control this thing
  That brings us all such disgrace,
It could do more good than anything else
  To make the world a better place.

  It forms beautiful music for us to hear.
  It carries our good news far and near.
  It can carry our love from city to city.
  It can make us feel pretty or make us seem witty.
  An integral part of most every college,
  It can educate us and give us knowledge.
  It can give us good taste and make us friends.
  It can guide our children and make amends.
  It can help us know what folks have to say.
  Millions of them are in use every day.

We should learn its power and learn its use,
  And learn it while we're young.
It's an awesome thing that we'd better control.
  That thing that's called a tongue.

# ADVICE

Two very old women were homeless and hungry.
  A penny they had not one.
The first had taken all advice that was offered.
  The other had taken none.

The moral is not to close your ears,
  Or ignore what advice is about.
*It's simply that you must trust in yourself*
  *When others remain in doubt.*

# A LETTER TO DAUGHTER

This book closes with a letter . . . a universal letter of thoughts, feelings and memories from a parent to his or her now-married daughter.

This letter is included as one step in helping you, as a daughter, to understand the feelings, emotions and conflicts that your mother and/or father have experienced (or will experience in the all-too-near future).

The author of this book recognizes that all parts of this letter will not be applicable to all parent/daughter relationships. Perhaps circumstances are such that one or both parents were not able to (or will not be able to) share some of the experiences expressed in this letter. If so, there may be a loss that is deeply felt by the parent(s) and/or by you. Perhaps the reading of this letter will provide some insight, understanding, and empathy for such loss.

*My Darling Daughter:*

*I remember the months before you were born and how I loved you even then . . . how I would have gladly given my life so you might have the joy of life. I remember the anxiety and anticipation of waiting and wondering. I remember the joy, the pride and the happiness I felt during the moments following your birth.*

*When I first held you in my arms I experienced that unconditional love that exists only between a parent and child . . . a love not predicated upon your pleasing me . . . a love that you had the inate ability to instill in me and every right to receive for the rest of your life.*

*When I first held you I felt a sense of awesome responsibility and a certain inadequacy or fear that I might in some way fail you. I felt the hope of all your tomorrows. I felt a deep commitment to you and your needs. I felt a closeness that could only exist with my very own child.*

*Every parent in the maternity ward shared a secret that they dare not say aloud . . . that theirs was the most beautiful baby on the floor. Of course, my dear, I smiled inside with the absolute knowledge that none could compare with you.*

*Your first smile, your first word, your first step were all as if no other person had ever accomplished such great feats. The pleasure of watching you, a part of me, grow, learn and develop into a toddler and pre-schooler seems now as only a fleeting moment in time, yet a precious moment that I shall always cherish.*

*I remember the reluctant excitement I had on your first day of school . . . the desire to see you develop your full potential mentally, physically and socially, yet the reluctance to let you go.*

*I knew the road to becoming a woman would be a long and often lonely one. I felt sadness over the disappointments that I knew were ahead for you, yet so much joy over the triumphs and happy times that, too, would be yours.*

73

*I wanted so to prepare you for the "rough and tumble" times of growing up — to prepare you for tragedies that certainly lie ahead; i.e., your best girlfriend would invite someone else to spend the night with her; the boy you like the best doesn't even know you exist; your teacher doesn't like you; you will be too young or too old; your body will be changing; your emotions won't stay constant; "the group" won't accept you. It seemed such a waste not to share with you all the things I had learned, yet I knew that you must learn and experience those things for yourself. The one thing that I could do for you was to let you know in every way I could that no matter how insignificant (or how great) the problem, you would* always *be loved.*

*I remember the anger that I hopefully repressed when you were done an injustice, whether real or imagined.*

*I remember the pain when I had to punish you and the anguish of wondering if the punishment would teach you the principles by which you need to live.*

*I remember the heavyhearted joy when you started into puberty. The realization that this was your last stage of childhood was almost too much. After all, you'll always be my little girl.*

*I remember the fun we had all through our relationship . . . the long talks — usually between 1 A.M. and 3 A.M.*

*I remember your first date and the panic I felt. Had I told you too much? Had I told you enough? Had I explained your responsibility? Did you take the money I gave you so you can phone if you need to? Never mind that his parents are taking you and bringing you home . . . things can go wrong, you know! I remember the relief when you were only five minutes late (the clock had just finished chiming nine o'clock).*

*I remember rejection when you were in junior high, but having been there myself I knew it would need to come. You needed time to find yourself. I didn't wear the right clothes or say the right things. I remember the admonitions; "Don't pick me up in the Chevrolet. If the new car isn't available I will walk".*

*I remember the overwhelming urge (for only a brief few moments) to cancel your birth certificate.*

*I remember the disbelief that my petite, 100 lb. daughter was "the fattest girl in my class".*

*I remember sympathy when your self-worth was at a low.*

*I remember the fog we were in during those short years of high school . . . the confusion — was I supposed to tell Janet that the meeting was at 7 o'clock — was it Rodger or Paul that asked you to return his call . . . dates, ballgames, tests, English papers, reports, books from the library.*

*I remember the pride and tears at your graduation. The family was in, gifts received and acknowledged. I remember the quiet . . . our little girl was growing up.*

*I remember long talks, giggles, confidences shared. We are friends. You are a woman.*

*I remember the anxiety when I learned that you had found "THE ONE" for you. Who is he? What is his background? Will he be good to you? Will he be good for you? Will he be dependable? Will he be faithful? etc., etc. After all, could anyone really be good enough for my little girl?*

*I remember the flurry — a wedding to plan. I have dreamed it would be a certain way, but I know it is yours and his to plan. I stand by only to ask "Do you want to consider doing . . . ?"*

*More tears of joy . . . beautiful bride, handsome husband. The combined feelings of joy, hope and loneliness were felt as a part of me begins a new life.*

*Time passes. Me a grandparent? It seems like only yesterday that you were born. What a wonderful gift to be able to relax and relive all the joys as nature's eternal cycle repeats itself.*

*Thank you, my darling, for bringing me such joy. You are a blessed gift and a wonderful friend. Thank you for being you.*